Proverbs and Politics

Proverbs and Politics

THE BIBLICAL FOUNDATION FOR RIGHTEOUS GOVERNING

Dr. Bruce K. Waltke

Designed by Ilan Rosen.

Chagall, Marc. *The Tribe of Issachar*. 1964. Stained glass windows. The Twelve Maquettes of Stained Glass Windows for Jerusalem/The Hadassah Hebrew University Medical Centre, Jerusalem.

Copyright © 2015 Dr. Bruce K. Waltke
All rights reserved.

ISBN: 1508436193
ISBN 13: 9781508436195

"Observe [the law] carefully, for this will show your wisdom and understanding to the nations, who will hear about all these decrees and say, 'Surely this great nation is a wise and understanding people.' What other nation is so great as to have their gods near them the way the LORD our God is near us whenever we pray to him? And what other nation is so great as to have such righteous decrees and laws as this body of laws I am setting before you today?"

— *Deuteronomy 4:6-8*

"Every thinking man, when he thinks, realizes that the teachings of the Bible are so interwoven and entwined in our whole civic and social life that it would be literally — I do not mean figuratively, but literally — impossible for us to figure what the loss would be if these teachings were removed. We would lose almost all the standards by which we now judge both public and private morals; all the standards toward which we, with more or less of resolution, strive to raise ourselves."

— *President Theodore Roosevelt*

"Ultimately a nation's exaltation depends on its piety and ethics, not on its political, military, and /or economic greatness. In its external affairs a sinful nation among other things breaks treaties, propagandizes, lies, and bullies weaker nations. In its internal affairs it allows its judicial system to break down so that criminals and sluggards are rewarded and good citizens are overtaxed and intimidated."

— *Dr. Bruce K. Waltke*

"The true glory of a nation lies in its righteousness rather than its wealth or power."

— *Michael V. Fox*

Introduction

In January of 2015, the American Renewal Project partnered with Governor Bobby Jindal (LA), Senator James Lankford (OK), and former Congressman J.C. Watts (OK) to host the inaugural *The Call to Serve: Issachar Political Training* for men and women in the ministry. Issachar Training was designed to encourage and equip pastors who are considering running for school board, county commissioner, city council, mayor or state or federal legislative positions in 2016.

Issachar Training was developed with the men and women of Issachar in mind (1 Chron. 12:32) who understood the troubling times they were in and acted to offer solutions in response. They rose to the challenge to lead their nation knowing the risks and dangers involved.

Like the times of Issachar, our nation faces a crisis of Biblical proportion. As a result of secularism, our religious liberties are in jeopardy, our nation is vulnerable to terrorist attacks from both inside and outside of our porous borders, our education, healthcare, and social welfare programs are in serious disrepair, our veterans and their families are suffering at great expense, and our children and grandchildren are saddled with unsustainable debt by our generation.

As Christians, we take full responsibility for allowing secularism to destroy our culture, society, and government; we ask God for mercy and forgiveness for what we Christians have allowed to happen to our nation.

To be a part of the solution we as Christians must turn to God, renewing our minds and hearts meditating on Biblical Wisdom. At the Issachar Training, we heard from the renowned Old Testament scholar, Dr. Bruce K. Waltke who taught the Biblical imperative that pastors must be involved in politics. Using key texts from the Book of Proverbs, he identified ways in which Christians can bring Salt and Light to all areas of society, including government and politics.

This text is based on Dr. Waltke's exegesis, designed to enable and invigorate men and women with Biblical Wisdom. Issachar Training seeks to train men and women to impart righteousness to our nation and restore American governance to its God-given purpose. Our call as Christians is not to "take our nation back," but to turn back to God and humbly serve our fellow citizens.

Pastors are already on the front lines of every cultural issue dealing with every area of life in which their congregants struggle. Being men of the Word, they are among the best suited to lead our country—for the wellbeing of all Americans.

The preamble to the Book of Proverbs states, "The Fear of the Lord is the foundation of true wisdom." What better way then to build a Biblical foundation for governance than beginning with proverbial instruction?

Dr. Waltke argues that the Book of Proverbs was written to make a nation righteous. May his words inspire and refresh you as you seek to apply Biblical ethics to restoring American governance.

Sincerely,
David Lane
The American Renewal Project

"Righteousness exalts a nation, but sin is a disgrace to any people."

— Proverbs 14:34

Table of Contents

THE FOUNDATION OF WISDOM 1

I. The Fear of the Lord 2
    a. The Revealed Word of the Lord 3
    b. Humility and Trust in God 4
    c. Five Actions Outlined in Proverbs 2 5

II. The Law of Moses 7

III. The Book of Proverbs 9
    a. The Struggle Between Right and Wrong is Inescapable 11
    b. If the Righteous Do Nothing, the Wicked Will Prevail 13
    c. God Holds Christians Responsible 14

IV. The Teachings of Jesus 17

FREQUENTLY RAISED OBJECTIONS TO CHRISTIAN POLITICAL ENGAGEMENT 19

    I.   Misunderstanding the First Amendment............20
    II.   Disordering Priorities..25
    III.   Misunderstanding Piety 26
    IV.   Avoiding Mud: Politics is a Dirty Business.........27
    V.   Avoiding Alienation..28

THE AMERICAN RENEWAL PROJECT'S CALL TO PASTORS.. 31

ENCOURAGEMENT FROM SENATOR JAMES LANKFORD 35

DEFINITION OF TERMS 41

BIBLIOGRAPHY 43

ABOUT THE AUTHOR... 47

The Foundation Of Wisdom

Pastors, who know the Bible better than most are in one of the best positions to apply Biblical ethics to govern America.

Mosaic Law, the Book of Proverbs, and Jesus's teachings provide a solid foundation for a national ethic that rightly guides a nation's moral behavior.

The foundation for a wise and righteous government can be likened to a four- layered cake where each layer is squarely laid one on top of the other. The Fear of the Lord provides the base upon which everything else rests. When combined, the Fear of the Lord, the Law of Moses, The Book of Proverbs, and Jesus's teachings provide the foundation for a wise and righteous government.

> Jesus's Teachings
>
> Wisdom from the Book of Proverbs
>
> The Law of Moses
>
> The Fear of the Lord

THE FEAR OF THE LORD

Ethical behavior is laid out in the Book of Proverbs' preamble: "The fear of the LORD is the beginning of knowledge, but fools despise wisdom and discipline" (Prov. 1:7). By "beginning," Solomon means *the* foundation; not merely a starting point, but that on which everything else depends.

> "*The fear of the Lord (yir-'at YHWH)* is the book's theological and epistemological foundation. The 'principal thing.'"

The fear of the Lord also pertains to special revelation revealed through the Bible, embodying **three inseparable thoughts:**

- The revealed Word of the Lord,
- The humble acceptance of that revelation, and
- Trusting that God upholds his revelation.

"There can be no reason for praying if there be no expectation of the Lord's answering." — Charles H. Spurgeon

The Revealed Word of the Lord

Psalm 19 equates "Fear of the Lord" as a synonym for Book of the Law, mediated by Moses:

- Law of the Lord (Perfect, refreshing the soul),
- Statutes of the Lord (Trustworthy, making wise the simple),
- Precepts of the Lord (Right, giving joy to the heart),
- Commands of the Lord (Radiant, giving light to the eyes),
- *Fear of the Lord* (Pure, enduring forever),
- Decrees of the Lord (Firm, and all of them are righteous), and
- Enduring forever.

"When the governments of nations are shaken with revolution, and ancient constitutions are being repealed, it is comforting to know that the throne of God is unshaken, and his law unaltered."
— Charles H. Spurgeon

Solomon identified his proverbs and the sayings of the wise (which he adopted and adapted to sound theology) as both the revealed Word of the LORD and as "the fear of the LORD": "If you accept my words … you will understand the fear of the

Lord and find the knowledge of God. <u>For the LORD gives wisdom; from his mouth come knowledge and understanding</u> (Prov. 2:1-6).

HUMILTY is another essential trait to fear the Lord. "The fear of the Lord teaches a man wisdom and humility comes before honor" (Prov. 15:33).

In the Sayings of Agur, the sage Agur confesses he cannot attain a reliable ethic on his own, acknowledging himself as a finite mortal. He says, *"I am the most ignorant of men; I do not have a man's understanding. I have not learned wisdom, nor have I knowledge of the Holy One"* (Prov. 30:2, 3).

Contrarily, postmodernism, which relies solely on human reason to establish an ethic for moral behavior, has been a colossal failure. From eugenics to genocide and ethnic cleansing, political leaders, educators, judges, humanitarians, and scientists now determine who lives, and at what point they can be legally experimented on and eventually extinguished. Today, no human life is assured as precious or safe—because the very premise of our laws—our God-given inalienable rights—is being destroyed.

Relying solely on human reason also results in a constantly changing value system, because human knowledge is limited. As more information is assessed and/or revealed what was previously thought as good and right later turns out to be quite foolish.

Humbly confessing that we as finite human beings cannot rightly behave without God, acknowledges the eternal truth that only God, as the creator of everything, can speak authoritatively about the righteousness he created.

By humbly accepting this revelation we can trust that God is true to His Word. "We must have a fixed point in order to judge," as Blaise Pascal rightly asserts.

TRUST comes from knowing "Every word of God is flawless; he is a shield to those who take refuge in him" (Prov. 30:5); "As for God, his way is perfect, the word of the Lord is flawless. It is a shield for all who take refuge in him" (Psalm 18:30).

Fearing the Lord Involves Five Actions Outlined in Proverbs 2

<u>First, Accept the Word of God.</u> This entails complete surrender, depending on God rather than leaning on our own understanding, what we think is right in our own eyes.

<u>Second, Store Up the Word.</u> This entails memorizing scripture with religious affection. We must store it in our hearts; in the locus of our thinking, emotions, and volition.

Consider the difference in character of the magi and the Jewish scribes Matthew describes in the account of Jesus's birth. The magi at first had only God's revelation in creation—a star— to guide them. But that star, revelation through creation, only enabled them to begin their journey, not complete it. To complete their journey to encounter Jesus, they needed revelation through God's Word. The Jewish scribes who had memorized God's word and were knowledgeable of Micah's prophecy, instructed the magi to find the Christ child in Bethlehem.

The magi found Christ by obeying only one verse of scripture because their hearts worshiped God. The Jewish scribes who had memorized most of scripture never found the savior of the world, because they did not have worshipping hearts; they loved themselves too much.

<u>Third, Listen to and Apply God's Word.</u> A humble heart turns its ear to hear the Word of God. Eusebius, a fourth century historian says of the Emperor Constantine, that he "stood hours to hear the word; replying, when asked to sit, 'that he thought it wicked to give negligent ears, when the truth handled as spoken of God'."

Constantine knew the first sign of rebellion against his rule was inattentiveness to his command. By standing and attentively listening, Constantine manifested humility needed to fear the Lord.

> *"Change, 'metanoia,'*
> *results not from 'will power'*
> *but from what Iris Murdoch calls,*
> *'a long deep process of unselfing.'"*

<u>Fourth, Call Out, Crying Aloud for God's Wisdom.</u> Earnestly seeking leads to fearing the Lord, expressing an insatiable appetite that only can be filled sacramentally with thanksgiving.

<u>Fifth, Look and Search for Wisdom</u> as if searching for hidden gold, silver, or precious stones.

> *"The Bible is no lazy man's book: much of its treasure,*
> *like the valuable minerals stored in the bowels of the earth,*
> *only yield up themselves to the diligent seeker."*
> — A.W. Pink

The Law of Moses

> *"The Book of the Law has had greater consequences*
> *for human history than any other single book.*
>
> *"Its regulations are the first to establish*
> *universal education and health for all members of a nation*
> *and fixes the only welfare system in existence during ancient times."*
> —Dr. Bruce K. Waltke

A nation's moral behavior must be based on the Covenant that God gave His chosen people at Sinai through Moses and later supplemented it in the Book of the Law, which comprises most of the Book of Deuteronomy. God instructed Moses, "Do not add to what I command you and do not subtract from it, but keep the commands of the LORD your God that I give you" (Deut. 4:2).

The fundamental principles guiding Israel's ethics and governance are detailed throughout the Book of the Law of Moses. Deuteronomy 17-18 includes a section on Israel's rulers; widely recognized as "Israel's constitution."

Israel's constitution clearly instructs priests to stand next to the judge while he ruled according to the Book of the Law (v. 8-9). Israel's constitution superseded any authority of any king God raised up (v. 18-20).

Which is why, King David instructed Solomon to obey the Book of the Law in 1 Kings 2:1-4, obliging all of Israel's future leaders to use the Book of the Law as the basis for their rule. Interestingly, the sayings of the wise were originally composed for future rulers, but the Book of Proverbs *democratizes them for all of Israel's youth.*

David told Solomon: "So be strong, act like a man, and observe what the LORD your God requires: Walk in obedience to him, and keep his decrees and commands, his laws and regulations, as written in the Law of Moses. Do this so that you may prosper in all you do and wherever you go" (1 Kings 2:2-3).

Solomon also provided further instruction about the Ten Commandments. For example, Proverbs 25:21 escalates the 6th Commandment's prohibition of murder by commanding: "If your enemy is hungry, give him food to eat; if he is thirsty, give him water to drink."

Proverbs 31:28, 29 mention how the husband stands up, presumably when his wife enters a public assembly (cf. Job 29:7—8), and publicly honors and praises his wife. His example escalates the 7th Commandment's prohibition to not commit adultery to honor your wife.

Likewise, in Proverbs 22:9 Solomon instructs positive, genuine action—to give—exceeding the 8th Commandment's prohibition of stealing. He says, "A generous man will himself be blessed, for he shares his food with the poor." Go beyond the law: be generous.

When considering the 9th Commandment, "You shall not bear false witness against your neighbor," Proverbs 10:12 warns, "Hatred stirs up dissention, but love covers over all wrongs." Solomon escalates, the command not to bear false witness to, "Protect your neighbor's reputation by drawing a veil over his or her wrongs; do not put them on the stage and then draw the curtain apart for all to see their faults."

The Book of Proverbs

"If the Book of the Law has had the greatest positive impact on Western culture than any other book, how much more would be the impact of wisdom gained from the Book of Proverbs?"
—Dr. Bruce K. Waltke

The Book of Proverbs was written to make a nation righteous and to know Wisdom: "… doing what is right and just and fair" (Proverbs 2:9).

By wisdom with reference to the creation is meant the immeasurable weights of wind and of the sea the trackless ways of lightning, and the complexities of the ecology. If the Lord with wisdom as his tool graciously accomplished the wonders of the various phases of creation—setting the earth on its foundations by splitting the primeval waters and setting the heavens in their appointed place and watering the earth with dew from its clouds—think what his revealed wisdom will do in the lives of those who find it.

Proverbs emphasizes that wisdom is centrally located in the public square. Wisdom shouts from the highest points along roads, crossroads, and cities' entrances. Wisdom is inseparable from every area of life.

Proverbs 8:1-3: "Does not wisdom call out? Does not understanding raise her voice? On the heights along the way, where the paths meet, she takes her stand; beside the gate leading into the city, at the entrances she cries aloud."

> *"Wisdom ... delivers her message where the competition is fiercest, not competition from other orators but from the everyday distractions of business, politics, and disputes. Far from being esoteric or academic, Wisdom plunges into the midst of this hustle and bustle to reach people where they are. The same accessibility is claimed for God's commandments in Deuteronomy 30:11-14."*
>
> —Michael V. Fox

The Proverbs emphasize that wisdom is inseparably correlated with righteousness. *If you are wise, you are righteous; if you are righteous, you are wise.*

Righteous behavior disadvantages self to advantage others, according to the ethical standards of God's word. Wicked behavior advantages self by disadvantaging others. Wickedness in

Proverbs is far subtler than the actions the Ten Commandments prohibit.

Murder, theft, adultery and lying are wicked—but so also is any conduct that disadvantages others to advantage self. Politicians accepting bribes for personal gain, knowing that voting in a particular way will harm citizens, is wicked. Voting to reduce legislators' excessive pensions may be righteous because it is most likely in their citizens' best interest.

Engaging in the political process furthers God's intention that the state be righteous, not wicked.

The Book of Proverbs emphasizes that the struggle for right and wrong is inescapable. There will always be a struggle between righteousness—serving others, and wickedness—serving self. Christians are required to fight for righteousness.

In Proverbs 1:8-9:18 ten parental lectures illustrate the struggle between wisdom and folly, between righteousness and wickedness.

Proverbs exhorts us to stay clear of easy money and easy sex, two things that will always actively tempt. ("On behalf of folly, wicked men offer fast money, and the adulteress, casual sex.")

Righteousness demands that financial gain/income be the reward of one's own work, not the plunder of another's earnings, and that sex be enjoyed within the responsibilities of marriage.

Christians are instructed not to "give in to sinful men." Proverbs 1:10 says, "My son, if sinners entice you, do not give in to them." Sinners love company; they tempt.

When the Supreme Court legitimized abortion, it sinned by violating the innocent's right to self-defense. When the Supreme Court legitimized homosexual cohabitation it sinned against God. Defending fruitless marriage that provides no offspring for future generations and in old age will require dependency on others for support harms society.

When legislators pass pork-barrel legislation to secure re-election and acquire more power, they sin. Godless politicians steal from the innocent, yoking citizens in bondage to debt and in slavery through subsistence living. Politicians sin when they campaign using negative attack ads, slinging mud at their opponents, violating the 9th Commandment "thou shall not bear false witness against your neighbor."

The Proverbs warn that sinners' politick aggressively to gain followers and cultural approval ("come along with us"). The simple-minded, that is to say, the open-minded or uncommitted, refer to youth who are not committed to Biblical truth and so can be swayed either towards righteousness or wickedness. Because the simpleton is open to both and has not committed himself to righteousness, the Proverbs consider him wicked (Prov. 1:20-33; 8:1-36).

The struggle for right and wrong is everywhere; at the city gate—involving the masses who can be swayed either way. This is why emphasizing Biblical values is essential to advancing wisdom and righteousness in a nation.

Because wisdom and folly are engaged in political struggle to win the allegiance of uncommitted youth, Christians must be also.

Christians cannot afford to avoid political involvement.

Thucydides admonished as such when orating to the Athenians about Pericles c. 490 B.C. He said, "Just because you do not take an interest in politics doesn't mean politics won't taken an interest in you."

The Proverbial parable of the sluggard and the vineyard warns that **unless the God-fearing contend for righteousness against the wicked, the wicked will prevail** (Prov. 24:30-34).

Society's natural state is self-serving, unless and until, selfless service to others overcomes it. In this parable, the vineyard represents inherited ethics and the morality of righteousness and its fruit. The sluggard, "someone who has no sense," represents the son who neglects wise instruction and in so doing destroys the vineyard and loses its beneficial fruit.

What is required to nurture a vineyard? 1) Forethought and preparation; 2) investment of time and energy, weeding, fertilizing the soil, placing vines in exact places, pruning, and overseeing irrigation; 3) diligent, painstaking labor to remove rocks and build stone walls, and creating and manning a watchtower to safeguard the vineyard; and 4) patience, waiting for several years even before the vines ever bear fruit.

What dangers must be considered to nurture the vineyard? 1) The field's natural state must be understood—does it yield inedible, non-nutritional weeds or painful thorns and thistles? 2) An accurate assessment must be conducted about the level of work required to cultivate and nourish healthy growth; and 3) Skill and ability to identify that which could destroy the vineyard from within its walls—weeds, root structure, pests, or thieves.

The parable illustrates similarities between society and the vineyard. Society's natural state does not produce righteousness, but wickedness. Human nature's depraved state results in self-serving selfishness and greed. And such wickedness is hostile and active. Danger exists within and without societal borders.

Ralph Waldo Emerson points out in *Man the Reformer* that, "every species of property is preyed upon by its own enemies."

Iron is ruined by rust; cloth, by moths; and meat, by putrefaction. Similarly, while the sluggard sleeps, wickedness is on the move to steal and destroy his inheritance.

Christians must recognize the consequences of remaining neutral, inactive, passive, or MIA: The wicked will plunder their heritage—because the wicked do not sleep and are vigilantly scheming.

God holds Christians responsible for their actions.

In the 25th saying of the Thirty Sayings of the Wise (Prov. 24:10-12) important parallels are drawn for Americans who have been given more blessings than anyone else on earth. Americans have a greater responsibility to seek righteousness and are held to a higher standard of accountability.

"If you falter in times of trouble, how small is your strength! Rescue those being led away to death hold back those staggering towards slaughter. If you say, 'But we knew nothing about this,' does not he who weighs the heart perceive it? Does not he who guards your life know it? Will he not repay each person according to what he has done?"

As Gary Haugen, founder and president of International Justice Mission articulates in *The Locus Effect*, bribed judges and brutal police forces in the Third World are as equally devastating as the great locust plague of the 1930s that destroyed America's heartland. Small, unforeseen locusts destroyed a primary food source, creating a chain reaction that led to a widespread economic crisis and exponential increases in poverty, starvation, and death.

Recognizing the destruction of the 1930s locust crisis and doing nothing about it is comparable to America's current crisis. As Dante remarked, *"The darkest places in hell are reserved for those who maintain their neutrality in times of moral crisis."*

Former Supreme Court Associate Justice William O. Douglas explains this well. He said: "As nightfall does not come all at once, neither does oppression. In both instances, there is a twilight when everything remains seemingly unchanged. And it is in such twilight that we all must be aware of change in the air however slight, lest we become unwitting victims of the darkness."

Like the 25th saying of the Thirty Sayings of the Wise (Prov. 24:10-12) the same truth is taught in Proverbs 31: 8, 9 and Isaiah 1:17:

> "Speak up for those who cannot speak for themselves, for the rights of all who are destitute. Speak up and judge fairly; defend the rights of the poor and needy;"

> "Learn to do right; seek justice. Defend the oppressed. Take up the cause of the fatherless; plead the case of the widow."

And as God warns in Ezekiel 3 and 33, Christians are held responsible for exposing wickedness and warning those who commit evil acts. If Christians,

> "Do not warn the wicked, or speak out to dissuade them from their evil ways in order to save their life, that wicked person will die for their sin, and I will hold you accountable for their blood. But if you do warn the wicked person and they do not turn from their wickedness or from their evil ways, they will die for their sin; but you will have saved yourself.

> "Again, when a righteous person turns from their righteousness and does evil, and I put a stumbling block before them, they will die. Since you did not warn them, they will die for their sin. The righteous things that person did will not be remembered, and I will hold you accountable for their blood. But if you do warn the righteous person not to sin and they do not sin, they will surely live because they took warning, and you will have saved yourself."

While we are culpable as a society, we are personally—individually—culpable, even within our own communities, for claiming ignorance, inaction, or indifference to evil.

We cannot claim, "We knew nothing about this," especially living in the multi-media age of the Internet in America. We are well aware that corrupt politicians are being elected and are recklessly spending and borrowing money, knowing such actions will bankrupt our children, grandchildren and great-grandchildren. Saddling future generations with unsustainable debt assures financial calamity.

Our omnipotent, omnipresent and omniscient God knows our every thought, word, and deed; and is just. He will punish us not only for what we have done but also for what we have left undone. "Be not deceived, God is not mocked; a man reaps what he sows."

As Plato warned, *"The price of apathy towards public affairs is to be ruled by evil men."*

Jesus Christ's teachings perfect the Law of Moses and the Book of Proverbs.

While sitting on a mountainside Jesus taught his disciples and the crowd the beatitudes, the purpose of being salt and light and explained how he himself was the fulfillment of the Law. He said, "Do not think that I have come to abolish the Law or the Prophets; I have not come to abolish them but to fulfill them" (Matt. 5:17).

Jesus also said, "Now something greater than Solomon is here" (Luke 11:31). And Hebrews' author attests, "Moses was faithful as a servant in all God's house," bearing witness to what would be spoken by God in the future. But Christ is faithful as the Son over God's house" (Hebrews 3:5,6).

Together, as a whole, the four layers of the cake (the Fear of the Lord, the Law of Moses, Wisdom from the Book of Proverbs, and Jesus's teachings) provide the essential ingredients necessary to strengthen genuine Christian faith and wisely guide a nation in righteousness.

Frequently Raised Objections To Christian Political Engagement

---

PASTORS HESITATE TO INVOLVE THEMSELVES in politics generally for five reasons. They:

1) Misunderstand the First Amendment and the history, purpose, and concept of the phrase, "separation of church and state,"

2) Claim to have "better priorities,"

3) Misunderstand piety,

4) Believe politics is a dirty business and don't want to get dirty, and

5) Are afraid that identifying and/or associating with a political party will alienate members of their church and/or create division within their community.

Misunderstanding the First Amendment

The First Amendment states that Congress shall make no law respecting an establishment of religion or prohibit the free exercise thereof. But within 175 years the Supreme Court in 1963 redefined the First Amendment's Establishment Clause reversing its original purpose and rejecting the Founding Fathers' intent. The Court ruled in an 8-1 decision that the government "shall allow no religious activity" in publicly funded activity, also prohibiting free exercise of religion in that public life. Against the will of 80 percent of the American people, the Supreme Court removed the Bible and prayer from public schools.

Lone dissenting Justice Potter Steward wrote, "[the decision] led not to true neutrality with respect to religion, but to the establishment of a religion of secularism."

Since 1963 Christian symbols have been increasingly disallowed on government property, ironically including the Ten Commandments, which were paramount to establishing the America legal system. The Supreme Court trivialized God by removing references to God and the Bible in ethical and moral discussions. The Court segregated the Church to a ghetto attempting to prohibit Christians from universally influencing public opinion.

The Court's ruling to disallow religious activity in government institutions and public life essentially created a false religion of secularism and created a secular state. Justice Potter Stewart continued in his dissent:

"If religious exercises are held to be an impermissible activity in schools, religion is placed in an artificial and state-created disadvantage.... And a refusal to permit religious exercises thus is seen, not as the realization of state neutrality, but rather as the establishment of a religion of secularism, or at least, as governmental support of the beliefs of those who think that religious exercises should be conducted only in private."

The Supreme Court's redefinition of the Establishment Clause flouted the Book of Proverb's repeated insistence: "My son, do not forget my teaching, but keep my commands in your heart."

Before 1963 public school education included teaching from the Book of Proverbs and the singing of hymns in assembly. The Court's ruling prohibits such previous teaching (although current Common Core curriculum is teaching Islam), which if violated can result in penalties for teachers and/or students.

"Forgetting" God's teaching in Hebrew, means more than a mental lapse; it is a moral lapse. In Hebrew the opposite of "to re-member" is not "to forget" but "to dismember." The Supreme Court effectually dismembered future generations of Americans from their Biblical heritage.

The Court dismembered its people from their roots.

The principles outlined in the Declaration of Independence and the Constitution are derived from the Bible. The concepts of "self-evident truths, all men created equal and endowed by their Creator with certain inalienable rights" are Biblical. These principles have led to unprecedented freedoms in a country unlike any other.

Consider the countries in which governments are not rooted in Biblical principles and where Jesus Christ is not preached. In India, Hinduism creates a caste system teaching its people their fate is tied to birth; some will always be poor and "less than," and vise versa. In China and Russia indescribable brutality has ruled by strictly enforcing no faith, no religion, no God. Dictators like Mao and Stalin killed approximately one third of their own people, nearly 100 million dead because their leaders proclaimed "no God." In Muslim majority countries, Islam legalizes the denigration of women and children and is actively institutionalizing slavery, violence, and genocide of non-Muslims worldwide.

Since 1963, many pastors have acquiesced to the Court's re-interpretation of the First Amendment. They've accepted the secular—and false—definition of "separation of church and state."

Researcher George Barna, of the Barna Institute and the American Culture and Faith Institute, recently reported that 90 percent of the theologically conservative pastors he polled affirm that the Bible speaks to cultural and political issues. However, when he asked them, *"Well, are you teaching your people what the Bible says about those issues?"* Barna says, "the numbers drop ... to less than 10 percent who say they will speak to it."

When asked what pastors were willing to do to encourage their congregants to engage in the political process, Barna remarks, "almost nothing." He surmises that the pastors he polled, "won't probably get involved in politics because it's very controversial. Controversy keeps people from being in the seats, controversy keeps people from giving money, from attending programs."

He adds pastors' "tendency is to say, *Well, that's not part of my mission; my mission is to bring in more people and to get them to understand certain things that I feel they should know.*"

Barna also suggests that seminaries do not train pastors "to get people engaged in [political issues.] They are taught just to exegete scriptures; they are taught something about the history of where those scriptures came from – but they are not prepared."

Another misunderstanding is that of some organized Christian religions (the Anabaptist, Mennonites, Quakers, Amish and 20th century Jehovah Witnesses). They interpret separation of church and state as not being involved in politics. They refuse to vote, carry arms or participate in most areas of civil government, believing that nonparticipation in government brings them closer to the kingdom of God. They point to Jesus's answer to Pilate: "My kingdom is not of this world. If it were, my servants would fight to prevent my arrest by the Jewish leaders. But now my kingdom is from another place" (John 18:36).

This perspective fails to take into account the whole Bible, contradicts its definition of the purpose of government and the Christian's responsibility to govern.

Within the context of God's providence and sovereignty over all things, including all governments, God established a realm in which his subjects obey him out of their love for him.

God created the state (government) to restrain evil and promote the wellbeing of its citizens—through the establishment and enforcement of his laws. The Apostle Paul explains, "Let everyone be subject to the governing authorities, for there is no authority except that which God has established. The authorities that exist have been established by God" and "are God's servants." "For the one in authority is God's servant for your good" (Rom. 13:1-7).

> *"People in modern democratic societies,*
> *which have more power placed in their hands ...*
> *have an even greater responsibility to check evil,*
> *although it is never easy."*
> —Jack Lundbom

Christians must also pray for their nation, offering "petitions, prayers, intercession and thanksgiving ... for all people—for kings and all those in authority, that we may live peaceful and quiet lives in all godliness and holiness" (1 Tim. 2:1, 2).

In America, "We the People" are the authority. "We the People" govern a constitutional republic and have the authority to legislate and govern. Our leaders rule, theoretically, by representing the will of those who elect them. And as Thomas Jefferson wrote, *"Can the liberties of a nation be thought secure when we have removed their only firm basis, a conviction in the minds of the people that these liberties are the gift of God? That they are not to be violated but with his wrath?"*

> *"If God established the State to re-*
> *strain evil and promote good,*
> *should not Christians, and especially their leaders,*
> *actively influence the government to pass laws that both*
> *restrain evil as defined by God and enable us to live*
> *peacefully and quietly in all godliness and holiness?"*
> —Dr. Bruce K. Waltke

The false dichotomy the Supreme Court created by separating church/faith from state/public affairs should not deter Christian political involvement. Instead, it should inspire Christians to do more. As Jesus said, "To whom much is given, much is required."

Disordering Priorities

Many pastors might argue that preaching the gospel and teaching about and/or being involved in politics is contradictory to their calling. They claim that involving themselves in politics distracts them, pulling them away from their primary purpose of evangelism.

To be sure, the Church's fundamental mission is to transform human consciousness through preaching the Gospel and making disciples of all nations. But the Church ought not to pit establishing the eternal, spiritual kingdom in the human heart against a temporal, political kingdom of God in government. She must not sin against God and neighbor by what she has left undone: not politicking for a State where the yeast of sexual anarchy cannot thrive.

Jesus depicts our ministry to restrain evil and promote good using the metaphors of salt and light.

We are to preserve that which is good by minimizing and slowing down the effects of evil; expose evil by shining light on it, and by being light in darkness, offering hope and better alternatives to existing policies.

Abraham Lincoln, largely on the basis of Biblical ethics, emancipated the slaves. The Rev. Martin Luther King Jr. quoted Jesus when arguing for equality, inspired millions, and effected significant improvements in many areas of civil rights.

It was pastors, their family members and congregants who founded numerous humanitarian agencies, hospitals, orphanages, schools and higher educational institutions including the Ivy League, and influenced national movements and two great awakenings.

The notion of not being involved in politics has been justified by likening politicking to shining brass on a sinking ship. When a ship is sinking, it is argued, the priority is to help as many people possible into lifeboats. There's no time to spend shining the brass.

But, our religious and political heritage in America is much more than shining brass. It has a track record of offering hope and giving life.

Misunderstanding Piety

Some pastors hesitate to involve themselves in politics because of their rightful focus on piety, on developing the spiritual life of God's saints. However, it is wrong to argue that in Christian baptism, whereby Christians die to the world and are raised to a new life focused on heaven, that the world refers exclusively to things that do not matter in light of death and eternity in contrast to those that do matter in that light.

Piety, a devotion to heavenly matters, makes us light and salt in politics. By our devotion to heavenly virtue and godly living we become by word and deed the light and salt we are called to be. We act politically to restrain evil and to promote the good of all people.

Avoiding Mud: Politics is a Dirty Business

Some pastors argue they don't want to get involved in politics because it's a dirty business and they don't want to get dirty, stuck in the mire of mudslinging. However, just because a political process is abused does not mean it should not be used. One cannot throw the baby out with dirty bathwater.

As the Latin phrase, *abusus non tollit usum,* states, we must remember, "abuse does not preclude proper use." Expect the political process to be abused, but don't draw the false conclusion that such abuse makes its proper use impossible.

"Christians are called upon through faith to clean up the political mess. In fact, would our country be in such a disastrous state if Christians had been responsibly involved in its governance?"
—Dr. Bruce K. Waltke

Be encouraged. The Holy Spirit acting through us is greater than the spirit acting against us.

We are assured by God that, "he who began a good work in you will carry it on to completion until the day of Christ Jesus." And, that we can do all things through Jesus who gives us strength (Phil. 1:6, 4:13).

To say that we cannot overcome evil in politics is unbelief, which we must overcome by faith, trust, and obedience in God.

Avoiding Alienation

Many pastors express fear and/or concern that identifying and/or associating with a political party will alienate members of their church, create division in their communities, or hindrances for nonbelievers.

To be sure, when "religious" politicians share the passions of the world and defend special interests they merely foster animosity and alienation.

But this is not Christian politics.

Christian politics can only be defined within the context of Biblical ethics and morals, not in terms of political allegiance. Political parties are necessary, but we cannot vote solely for a political party instead of voting for those who advocate Biblical values. However, Christians also are required to establish righteousness within political parties.

Pastors must be involved in politics because God requires all Christians "to seek the peace and prosperity of the city" in which they live—by imparting righteousness through wisdom-based Biblical living.

The alternative to "doing nothing" enables the wicked, already on the move, to gain further ground. And as John Stuart Mill warned, *"The only thing necessary for the triumph of evil is for good men to do nothing."*

Christians also must vigilantly advocate now for righteousness to avoid future martyrdom. We already see the "elite," both in government and the news media, attacking freedom of speech and freedom of religion.

As Pastor Martin Niemoeller, leader of the German Confessing Church during Nazi occupation lamented, Christian impotence was costly. He said:

> "First they came for the socialists, and I did not speak out—because I was not a socialist. Then they came for the trade unionists, and I did not speak out—because I was not a trade unionist. Then they came for the Jews, and I did not speak out—because I was not a Jew.
>
> "Then they came for me—And there was no one left to speak for me."

Pastors are not obliged to demand a religious conversion, but we are obliged to demand a civil convergence.

As Peter Leithart argues, "Christian capitulation to secular politics – more the rule than the exception in the modern church – is nothing less than apostasy, a denial of the gospel that announces Jesus as Lord."

"Like a muddied spring or a polluted well are the righteous who give way to the wicked" (Prov. 25:26).

The American Renewal Project's Call To Pastors

THE BOOK OF THE LAW, the Book of Proverbs and Jesus's teachings provided the foundation for early Christians and New Testament believers to understand God's purpose for government and their role as citizens, slaves, or refugees.

Consider the example of the Apostle Paul, who was imprisoned numerous times for preaching the gospel. As a Roman citizen, Paul was due certain civil liberties by right of birth. This is why he claimed his rights under Roman law (*"I appeal to Caesar"* Acts 25:11).

Paul's recognition of Caesar's authority revealed three things. First, he believed and trusted in the Sovereign God, maker of heaven and earth. Second, he knew who he was—a humble servant saved by grace and chosen by God to bring the gospel to the Jews, Gentiles, and the Gentile government.

Third, Paul understood God's design for order; knowing that the government was God's earthly instrument to restrain evil, promote good, and administer justice.

He knew government served God's purposes and submitted to God's authority, saying: "Let everyone be subject to the governing authorities, for there is no authority except that which God has established. The authorities that exist have been established by God" (Romans 13:1).

Throughout Paul's writings he expressed his obedience to follow Christ, ready to gain his heavenly reward and leave his earthly prison. When confronted with death, his earthly choices for deliverance included 1) stop preaching the gospel, 2) surrender his civil rights to the Roman authorities, or 3) surrender himself to his Jewish accusers. He chose none of the above. He chose life in the face of death—*by choosing not to give up his rights.*

He chose to claim his legal rights by appealing to Caesar— knowing these rights existed solely because of God.

Paul not only appealed to Caesar, he appealed to his fellow citizens knowing that righteousness exalts a nation. He reasoned with them in the public square using their language and cultural references (Acts 17).

He also appealed to fellow believers encouraging them to live a life worthy of their calling (the Ephesians, Thessalonians, Corinthians, Romans, Galatians, Philippians, and Timothy, among others). He petitioned his fellow believers, sometimes in great despair, to pray for him, "lest he have sorrow upon sorrow."

Paul knew from the Proverbs, the Book of the Law, and from Jesus's teachings that every area of life is spiritual. The government, the public square, and all liberties and freedoms do not exist apart from God.

There will always be a tension between "the now and not yet," between a Christian's weariness with political battles and the longing for our Heavenly home. Yet in the meantime, we work within the system provided for us however corrupt it may be. Paul's appeal to the government of his day evidences that today Christians, and especially pastors, must do likewise.

The Book of Proverbs warns that a struggle between good and evil will always exist and therefore instructs believers to be prepared and learn how to live rightly in light of this struggle.

In the face of evil, under Soviet occupation, Pope John Paul II told his people: "Remember who you are. You are a Christian people."

Under Nazi occupation, Ronald Greer in *Living with Integrity*, writes about a conversation between fearful Dutch Christians and a former missionary Hendrik Kraemer. They asked Kraemer, "What should we do? How are we to live in such darkness?" He responded, "I cannot tell you what to do but I can tell you who you are. If you know who you are, then you will know what to do."

Then Kraemer read to them the words Peter gave to the early first century Christians who were afraid for their lives, witnessing and experiencing extreme persecution. Peter told them, "But you are a chosen people, a royal priesthood, a holy nation, God's special possession, that you may declare the praises of him who called you out of darkness into his wonderful light" (1 Pet. 2:9).

They thanked Kraemer, left, and started the Dutch underground resistance.

In the 21st Century and in a representative form of government, we as American Christians must appeal to "We the People." Our appeal, to our fellow citizens, government officials, and people of faith, is not a call to arms "to take our nation back." Our call is to prayerfully and humbly to turn to God, seek his guidance, protection, and correction to heal our land.

And we boldly claim God's promise given in 2 Chron. 7:14: "If my people, who are called by my name, will humble themselves and pray and seek my face and turn from their wicked ways, then I will hear from heaven, and I will forgive their sin and will heal their land."

Wisdom calls out from the highest points of the cities to the center of commerce and the public square. We must welcome it and discern how to impart it to every area of life.

How will you answer Wisdom's call?

Encouragement from Senator James Lankford

JAMES LANKFORD WAS SWORN IN as a United States Senator on January 3, 2015 after serving four years in the U.S. House of Representatives for Oklahoma's 5th district. Prior to running for office, from 1996 to 2009 he was the student ministries and evangelism specialist for the Baptist General Convention of Oklahoma and director of youth programming at the Falls Creek Baptist Conference Center in Davis, Oklahoma.

He resigned from his position on September 1, 2009 and says of this time, "From the beginning I did not sense that God was calling me to run [for office]. Running was the interview. He called me to the task. The campaign wasn't some vehicle in that. That was my responsibility to do and to do well."

Senator James Lankford Remarks:
The Call to Serve: Issachar Political Training Conference
Baton Rouge, Louisiana January 24, 2015

I've met other people who've had a journey like [mine] with God. They try to figure out how to process this. It is not uncommon for us in ministry to meet a tax collector who becomes a minister. But it is a little like "man bites dog" when a minister becomes a tax collector. We don't receive well men who step out of "ministry" into the "secular."

When I first ran for Congress I heard over and over again from people, "You're leaving the ministry." I responded, "I am not leaving the ministry. Jesus called me to follow him. This is what he called me to do. If I do something else I am disobeying him.

"I am still following him."

Nehemiah chapter one provides a foundation for people in ministry who are considering entering politics. In the first three verses, Nehemiah writes:

> "… while I was in the citadel of Susa, Hanani, one of my brothers, came from Judah with some other men, and I questioned them about the Jewish remnant that had survived the exile, and also about Jerusalem. They said to me, "Those who survived the exile and are back in the province are in great trouble and disgrace. The wall of Jerusalem is broken down, and its gates have been burned with fire."

The people are doing terrible. It's been 150 years since Babylon decimated Jerusalem (read the beginning of Ezekiel to get an understanding of how bad it was) and now the Medes and the Persians have inherited Babylonian slaves. It's also been 150 years since Nehemiah's family lived in Jerusalem. He didn't know where his family had lived and had never been to Jerusalem.

Nehemiah was the king's slave and cupbearer tasked with tasting all drinks before the king drank, to protect him from being poisoned. Nehemiah was expendable; not a trusted advisor. When he hears the news of Jerusalem he says in verses 4-11:

> "When I heard these things, I sat down and wept. For some days I mourned and fasted and prayed before the God of heaven. Then I said:
>
> 'LORD, the God of heaven, the great and awesome God, who keeps his covenant of love with those who love him and keep his commandments, let your ear be attentive and your eyes open to hear the prayer your servant is praying before you day and night for your servants, the people of Israel. I confess the sins we Israelites, including myself and my father's family, have committed against you. We have acted very wickedly toward you. We have not obeyed the commands, decrees and laws you gave your servant Moses.
>
> 'Remember the instruction you gave your servant Moses, saying, 'If you are unfaithful, I will scatter you among

the nations, but if you return to me and obey my commands, then even if your exiled people are at the farthest horizon, I will gather them from there and bring them to the place I have chosen as a dwelling for my Name.

'They are your servants and your people, whom you redeemed by your great strength and your mighty hand. Lord, let your ear be attentive to the prayer of this your servant and to the prayer of your servants who delight in revering your name. Give your servant success today by granting him favor in the presence of this man.'"

We learn three things from Nehemiah.

First, <u>Nehemiah was given a very specific burden.</u> It was only for him.

Second, <u>the problem in Jerusalem was spiritual.</u> Immediately Nehemiah recognized this. "We have disobeyed," he said. The city was in destruction—but it was a spiritual issue.

Third, <u>the problem and solution looked secular but it was of God.</u> Those of us in the ministry teach about the sacred and the secular. Many label activities as "That's ministry;" or "That's secular." Nehemiah blows that up. What was Nehemiah's task? To rebuild the wall, establish a functioning government to replace that which had collapsed, and get people out of debt. Which of these looked sacred? All of them.

Compare Nehemiah's calling with Ezra's. Ezra was tasked with finding priests and rebuilding the temple; definitely a spiritual task.

But what about Nehemiah? Were his tasks spiritual? Yes. That was God's call on him and God had to fulfill it or it would not occur.

We must be attentive to the times when we say, "that's secular" when it's actually God at work doing things that only God can do.

When people criticize a minister running for office I ask, "Does God care about government?"

Consider that all but possibly two of the Old Testament books (Job and maybe Ruth) were written by a political leader, to a political leader, or about a political leader.

And what was Saul's calling? God said, "He is my chosen instrument to the Jews, the Gentiles, and the Gentile kings." God was very specific. He was going to redo government through Saul.

God is at work in places you would not have expected. His ministry goes where God places you.

On Christmas Day 2013 I had the opportunity to lead a member of Congress to Christ. This past year I had the opportunity to lead a lobbyist to Christ. And this week as I was presiding over the Senate, I had the opportunity to share my testimony with a senior Senator. I was laying out the gospel to another senator on the dais of the United States Senate.

That doesn't happen unless God does it. We must break through the secular/sacred perspective and reject this assumption that God only works in certain occupations and doesn't work in others.

Follow what God wants you to do. Don't get ahead of him. Follow him.

"Wait for the LORD; be strong and take heart and wait for the LORD" (Psalm 27:14).

Definition of Terms

Ethics: An aspect of philosophy that involves systematizing, defending, and recommending concepts and rules of right and wrong conduct based on an external source generally applied to civil affairs.

God: The Christian God of Abraham, Isaac and Jacob, who created humankind in his image, inspired the Bible, and manifested himself in human flesh as the incarnate Lord Jesus Christ. This meaning of God was understood and assumed by most of America's Founding Fathers.

Morals: An individual's belief system about right and wrong attitudes and behavior.

Politics: Debate, conflict, compromise, negotiation, and struggle for power among individuals who hold opposing ethical and moral views and must work together in government. The Oxford Dictionary defines politics as, "the activities associated with the governance of a country or other area, especially the debate or conflict among individuals or parties having or hoping to achieve power."

Secular: An ethic that is not justified or argued in terms of religious belief, or an ethic that is only justified by its opposition to those who hold religious beliefs.

Bibliography

All scripture is from the New International Version.

Barker, Kenneth L. *The NIV Study Bible, New International Version*. Grand Rapids, Mich., U.S.A.: Zondervan Bible Publishers, 1985.

Barna, George. "'Pastors Preaching about Politically Controversial Issues' on *Today's Issues*, American Family Radio." Telephone interview with Mark Wildmon. July 31, 2014.

Douglas, William O., and Melvin I. Urofsky. *The Douglas Letters: Selections from the Private Papers of Justice William O. Douglas*. Bethesda: Adler & Adler, 1987.

Durling, Robert M., and Ronald Martinez. *The Divine Comedy of Dante Alighieri*. Section 1 The Inferno. New York: Oxford University Press, 1996.

Emerson, Ralph Waldo. "Man the Reformer." A Lecture read before The Mechanics' Apprentices' Library Association, Boston, January 25, 1841.

Fox, Michael V. *Proverbs 1-9: A New Translation with Introduction and Commentary*. New York: Doubleday, 2000.

Fox, Michael V. *Proverbs 10-31: A New Translation with Introduction and Commentary.* New Haven: Yale University Press, 2009.

Gordon, David J. *Iris Murdoch's Fables of Unselfing.* Columbia: University of Missouri Press, 1995.

Greer, Ronald. *Living with Integrity.* Nashville: Abington Press, 2009.

Haugen, Gary, and Victor Boutros. *Locust Effect: Why the End of Poverty Requires the End of Violence.* Oxford; New York: Oxford University Press, 2013.

Jefferson, Thomas. "Notes on the State of Virginia." Richmond: Randolph, 1853.

Jowett, Benjamin. *The Portable Plato: Protagoras, Symposium, Phaedo, and the Republic; Complete, in the English Translation of Benjamin Jowett.* New York: Viking Press, 1948.

Leithart, Peter J. *1 & 2 Kings Brazos Theological Commentary on the Bible.* Grand Rapids, Mich.: Brazos Press, 2006.

Lundbom, Jack R. *Jeremiah 1-20: A New Translation with Introduction and Commentary.* New York: Doubleday, 1999.

Lundbom, Jack R. *Jeremiah 21-36: A New Translation with Introduction and Commentary.* New York: Doubleday, 2004.

Lundbom, Jack R. *Jeremiah 37-52: A New Translation with Introduction and Commentary.* New York: Doubleday, 2004.

Mayer, Milton. *They Thought They Were Free: The Germans, 1933-45.* Chicago: University of Chicago Press, 1955.

Mill, John Stuart. "Inaugural Address." Lecture, from The University of St. Andrews, St. Andrews, Scotland, February 1, 1867.

Paul, C. Kegan. *The Thoughts of Blaise Pascal, Translated from the Text of M. Auguste Molinier.* London: George Bell and Sons, 1901.

Pink, Arthur Walkington. *The Life of David.* Grand Rapids: Zondervan Pub. House, 1958.

Roosevelt, Theodore. "The Influence of the Bible." 1901 address to the Long Island Bible Society, in Reisner, Christian F. *Roosevelt's Religion.* New York: Abingdon Press, 1922.

School District of Abington Township, Pennsylvania, et al. v. Edward Schempp, et al.; Murray, et al. v. Curlett, et al., Constituting the Board of School Commissioners of Baltimore City, 374 U.S. 203 83 S. Ct. 1560; 10 L. Ed. 2d 844; 1963 U.S. LEXIS 2611

Spurgeon, C.H. *The Treasury of David: Containing an Original Exposition of the Book of Psalms, a Collection of Illustrative Extracts from the Whole Range of Literature, a Series of Homiletical Hints upon Almost Every Verse, and Lists of Writers upon Each Psalm.* London: Passmore and Albaster, 1871.

Thucydides. "Pericles' Funeral Oration." After The Peloponnesian War, Athens, c.490 B.C.

Waltke, Bruce K., and Cathi J. Fredricks. *Genesis: A Commentary.* Grand Rapids, Mich.: Zondervan, 2001.

Waltke, Bruce K. *The Book of Proverbs: Chapters 1-15.* Grand Rapids, Mich.: William B. Eerdmans Pub., 2004.

Waltke, Bruce K. *The Book of Proverbs: Chapters 15-31.* Grand Rapids, Mich.: William B. Eerdmans Pub., 2005.

Whybray, R. Norman. *The Making of the Pentateuch A Methodological Study.* London: Bloomsbury Publishing, 1987.

About the Author

Dr. Bruce K. Waltke
Houghton College, AB; Dallas Theological Seminary, ThM, ThD; Harvard University, PhD.

Dr. Bruce Waltke, a preeminent Old Testament scholar, holds a doctorate in Greek and New Testament from Dallas Theological Seminary and a doctorate in Ancient Near Eastern Languages and Literature from Harvard. His teaching career, spanning Dallas Theological Seminary, Regent College, Reformed Theological Seminary, and Westminster Theological Seminary won him a reputation of being a master teacher with a pastoral heart. Dr. Waltke also pastored several churches, lectured at many evangelical seminaries in North America and has spoken at numerous Bible conferences.

He is a member of the Committee of Bible Translation of the New International Version and helped translate the New American Standard Version. He served as editor for the *Theological Word Book of the Old Testament*, *The New International Dictionary of Old Testament Theology and Exegesis*, *The New Geneva Study Bible*, *Spirit of the Reformation Study Bible*, as the Old Testament editor for the *Expositor's Bible Commentary* series.

He served as president of the Evangelical Theological Society and is an honorary member of the committee responsible for Today's New International Version.

Waltke's books include *Intermediate Hebrew Grammar, Introduction to Biblical Hebrew Syntax, Finding the Will of God, Creation and Chaos*, and commentaries on The Book of Proverbs and Micah.

He received an ECPA Christian Book Award in 2008 for *An Old Testament Theology: An Exegetical, Canonical,* and *Thematic*

Approach. He and C.J. Fredricks won the 2002 Gold Medallion Book Award for *Genesis* (Zondervan 2001).

J.I. Packer and Sven K. Soderland wrote a book in honor of Waltke, entitled *The Way of Wisdom: Essays in Honor of Bruce K. Waltke* (Zondervan, 2000).

Made in the USA
San Bernardino, CA
28 January 2020